LINCOLN MOTOR CARS
1920 THROUGH 1942
PHOTO ARCHIVE

LINCOLN MOTOR CARS
1920 THROUGH 1942
PHOTO ARCHIVE

Photographs from the Detroit Public Library's
National Automotive History Collection

Edited with introduction by Mark A. PatrickCurator,
National Automotive History Collection

Iconografix
Photo Archive Series

Iconografix
PO Box 609
Osceola, Wisconsin 54020 USA

Library of Congress Card Number 96-76227

ISBN 1-882256-57-3

96 97 98 99 00 01 02 03 5 4 3 2 1

Digital imaging by Pixelperfect, Madison, Wisconsin
Cover design by Lou Gordon, Osceola, Wisconsin

Printed in the United States of America

US book trade distribution by Voyageur Press, Inc. (800) 888-9653

PREFACE

The histories of machines and mechanical gadgets are contained in the books, journals, correspondence, and personal papers stored in libraries and archives throughout the world. Written in tens of languages, covering thousands of subjects, the stories are recorded in millions of words.

Words are powerful. Yet, the impact of a single image, a photograph or an illustration, often relates more than dozens of pages of text. Fortunately, many of the libraries and archives that house the words also preserve the images.

In the *Photo Archive Series,* Iconografix reproduces photographs and illustrations selected from public and private collections. The images are chosen to tell a story—to capture the character of their subject. Reproduced as found, they are accompanied by the captions made available by the archive.

The Iconografix *Photo Archive Series* is dedicated to young and old alike, the enthusiast, the collector and anyone who, like us, is fascinated by "things" mechanical.

The Lelands and Fords at Lincoln Motor Company. Left to right: Henry Leland, Mrs. and Mr. Edsel Ford, Mrs. and Mr. Henry Ford, Mrs. and Mr. Wilfred Leland. Photo taken at the closing of the sale to Ford Motor Company.

INTRODUCTION

Organized in 1920, Lincoln Motor Company was successor to a company of the same name founded in 1917 by Henry Martyn Leland and his son Wilfred Leland. Henry Leland was a master machinist who contributed greatly to the early successes of Oldsmobile and Cadillac. Credited with developing the industry's first commercially successful V-8 engine and introducing the electric self-starter, Leland has been called the American Sir Henry Royce. Leland was a principled man, of the sort seldom known in our time. He greatly admired Abraham Lincoln, and when Leland left Cadillac and General Motors to build Liberty engines under contract to the US government, he chose to name the business in Lincoln's honor. When the war ended, the market for Liberty engines evaporated. The Lelands were left with a modern factory, but no viable product. Within a brief span of time, the Lelands raised the capital to begin automobile manufacture.

To power their new motor car, the Lelands drew upon their experiences at Cadillac and designed a distinctly different, smoother-running V-8 of greater output. The first Lincoln, the Model L, appeared in the fall of 1920. Although highly regarded for its mechanics, the Model L was criticized for its lackluster coachwork. Sales suffered. The impact of the economic depression that followed World War I was perhaps equally detrimental to sales. As if feeble sales and a weak economy were not problems enough, Lincoln Motor Company faced the threat of a multi-million dollar tax claim on the war profits of its predecessor. In November 1921, Lincoln Motor Company entered into voluntarily receivership and, on February 4, 1922, was purchased by Ford Motor Company.

Henry Ford and Henry Leland were ill-suited as partners. Both were gifted, self-taught craftsmen, with strong personalities. They had previously worked together at Detroit Automobile Company, antecedent to the Cadillac Motor Car Company. Ford, who served as chief engineer, was apparently offended by Leland's criticism of his work. Ford left Detroit Automobile Company soon after Leland arrived. Ford may well have harbored ill feelings toward Leland. For whatever reasons, soon after Ford took control of Lincoln, both Henry and Wilfred Leland were either removed or resigned from Lincoln Motor

Company. Direction of Lincoln fell to Edsel Ford, in retrospect the perfect caretaker. His keen senses of design and marketing served the marque well. In 1922, bolstered by Ford's economic backing, more appealing coachwork (see paragraph that follows), and a revitalized economy, Lincoln sales more than doubled from those of its first year in production.

As stated, early Lincolns were criticized for their mundane coachwork. Built to Leland's order by Murray, the bodies were unquestionably of quality but lacking in style. Even before Edsel Ford took charge of Lincoln, steps were taken to improve the styling of Lincoln coachwork. A variety of bodies from Brunn, Fleetwood, and Judkins were catalogued. By the mid-1920s and throughout the custom body-era, Lincoln's sported semi-custom and custom coachwork by such notable American coachbuilders as Dietrich, Holbrook, LeBaron, Locke, Murphy, and Willoughby. Unquestionably, their elegant designs contributed greatly to Lincoln's success.

The early Model L was offered with either a 130-inch or 136-inch wheelbase chassis. The engine, a 357.8 cubic inch V-8, was rated at 81 brake horsepower, increased to 90 bhp by Ford. Additional changes in features and mechanics followed the takeover gradually. In 1923, the 130-inch wheelbase chassis was dropped; the engine head was modified to improve cooling; aluminum pistons replaced the original iron pistons; and four-wheel brakes were introduced. Although refinements and modifications were ongoing throughout its production, the next significant change to the Model L did not follow before 1928, when engine displacement was increased to 384.8 cubic inches.

In 1931, the Model K replaced the Model L. Built on a 145-inch wheelbase chassis, the Model K featured an improved 384.8 cubic inch V-8, rated at 120 bhp, and three-speed transmission with synchronized second and third gears. A lower, more streamlined appearance was possible, as the K featured a lower seating position and reduced wheel diameter from those of the L. The Model K was produced for one year only. It sold in fewer numbers than did the Model L, although this was most likely due to the deepening economic depression. In 1932, the Models KB and KA were introduced. The KB, built on a 145-inch wheelbase chassis, was powered by a new 447.9 cubic-inch 150 bhp V12. The KA, built on a 136-inch chassis, featured the 384.8 V-8 carried-over from the Model K, but with a boost to 125 bhp. This was the last year for Lincoln's V-8, as the 1933 KA was equipped with a new 381.7 cubic inch V-12.

Lincoln's adoption of the V-12 was, no doubt, a response to market forces. Competition, for the shrinking luxury car market, was intense during the Depression. Cadillac, even then Lincoln's staunchest rival, introduced a V-16 in 1930 and a V-12 in 1931. Marmon introduced a V-16 in 1931. Auburn, Packard, and Pierce-Arrow joined Lincoln in introducing a V-12 in 1932; Franklin followed in 1933. Somewhat a Johnny-come-lately, Lincoln was, nonetheless, committed to the 12-cylinder engine. While Cadillac dropped the V-12 after 1937 and the V-16 after 1940, and Packard dropped their V-12 after 1939, Lincoln offered nothing but V-12s through the 1948 model year. (Auburn, Franklin, Marmon, and Pierce Arrow had all expired by the end of 1937.)

The KA and KB Lincoln remained in production through 1933. The 1934 Lincoln was again designated the Model K, with 136-inch wheelbase cars defined as Series 521 and 145-inch wheelbase cars as Series 271. The former was used primarily for production and semi-production cars; the latter for custom and semi-custom cars. Each carried the same new V-12, a 414 cubic-inch engine rated at 150 bhp. The Model K remained in production through 1939, with few mechanical changes.

Production of the Model K had dwindled from a high of 3,024 in 1934 to 133 in 1939. The decline paralleled the world-wide deterioration in sales of semi-custom and custom-bodied motor cars. Fortunately, before 1939, Edsel Ford had realized that a smaller, less-costly Lincoln was required to insure the marque's survival. Ford may actually have been prompted to action by Briggs Manufacturing Company, the coachbuilder for Ford Motor Company. Briggs, seeking to increase its volume of work, employed John Tjaarda, a Dutch-born designer educated as an aeronautical engineer. As early as 1932, Tjaarda set to work on the design of what proved to be a revolutionary new Lincoln—the Zephyr.

The Zephyr's ultra-streamlined appearance and unit-body design were unique. A new Ford-designed V-12 was installed in the Zephyr and the car was offered in 1936 in two and four-door versions. Zephyr was an immediate success. Production for the 1936 model year fell a handful of units shy of 15,000. In 1937, four styles, including the six-passenger Town Limousine were offered, and production doubled from the previous year. Two and four-door convertibles were added to the Zephyr line in 1938. Zephyr was restyled in 1940 and, with the demise of the Model K, it alone carried the name of Lincoln.

Although the Zephyr was an unqualified success, it was its offspring, the Continental, that proved to be one of the most acclaimed automobiles of the 20th Century. Originally built as a one-off motor car for Lincoln's most valued customer, Edsel Ford, the Zephyr Continental Cabriolet (the Zephyr name was dropped in 1941) entered production in late 1939 for the 1940 model year. A coupe was later introduced for 1940. The Continental was, truly, an overnight sensation. Although production was limited, it boosted the image of Lincoln to an unprecedented level. The fact that the Continental name remains in use 50 years afterwards speaks volumes about its significance to Lincoln.

The limited-production Custom was the final Lincoln model to appear prior to 1942. Introduced in 1941, the Custom's 138-inch wheelbase and V-12 engine befit the seven-passenger sedan and limousine coachwork for which they were designed. Intended as a successor to the Model K, the Custom was little more than a stretched Zephyr. Hardly exciting, the Custom was, nonetheless, a Lincoln. Production of the Custom, as well as that of Zephyr and Continental, was cut short in February 1942, by the demands of war production. Of the three models, only Zephyr and Continental returned to production in 1946, and only Continental would carry the same nameplate.

Lincoln Motor Cars 1920 through 1942 Photo Archive and its companion *Lincoln Motor Cars 1942 through 1960 Photo Archive* celebrate one of the remaining titans of the automobile industry. With each, the reader can expect a glorious photographic history of some of the greatest American automobiles ever produced. The photographs are a part of the Detroit Public Library's National Automotive History Collection. The mission of the NAHC is to retain and preserve the historical record of the automobile and other forms of wheeled transportation. Toward this aim, the NAHC has become the premier collection of its type. Our files include 350,000 pieces of sales literature and 250,000 photographs. The collection also houses biographical files, books, magazines, art, blueprints, owner's manuals, and personal papers of automotive pioneers and trailblazers. Much of this material is unique. Most importantly, it is in the public library, and, therefore, is accessible to the enthusiast.

I offer special thanks to Michael Lamm, David R. Holls, Byron D. Olsen, and NAHC Librarian Serena Gomez, for their assistance in identification and for their useful suggestions.

View of the Lincoln Motor Company headquarters, with a statue of Abraham Lincoln, circa 1922. The statue was later removed to the Detroit Public Library, where it still stands.

The Lincoln Motor Company factory.

Woodworkers at the Lincoln Motor Company factory.

L-Series

1921 through 1930

A host of 1921 Model 101 Seven-Passenger Touring cars inside the Lincoln factory.

W.W. "Bill" Bramlette at the wheel of his 1921 *Lincoln Road Runner.*

BRAMLETTE WINS BIG NEVADA 1000-MILE ROAD RACE

Inyo County is represented in the first annual 1000-mile road race, conducted by the Nevada Highway Association, which began Wednesday and ends today. W. W. Bramlette of Little Lake, noted for his recent daring drive from Los Angeles to Bishop, when he covered the 283 miles of desert and mountain road in 6 hours and 38 minutes, is in the race to bring home the prize money.

The first division of the race takes the drivers to Elko by way of Wadsworth, Fallon, Lovelock, Imlay, Winnemucca, Golconda, Battle Mountain and Carlin; the next to Tonopah through Wells, Currie, Ely, Butlers, Locks Ranch, Hot Creek and Cliffords, and thence on to Reno via Mina, Hawthorne, Schurz, Yerington, Wellington, Gardnerville, Minden, Carson City and Steamboat Springs.

Concerning the Bramlette brothers, the Tonopah Times of last Saturday says:

At 8:30 yesterday morning the Lincoln road racer manned by the Bramlette brothers, left for Reno to complete logging the second half of the 1000-mile route of the proposed road race. W. W. acts as chauffeur and Walter E. is mechanician. The car is a stock car which attracted great attention during the stay in Tonopah, especially as it is known to hold the record for the road race from Los Angeles to Phoenix, Ariz., a distance of 424 miles, which was covered in 12 hours and 16 minutes. They also established a record from Los Angeles to Bishop, making the 283 miles in 6 hours and 38 minutes.

Reno Nev 510P July 1 1921

THE INDEX
Bishop Calif
I just won the hardest road race ever pulled in the world, the Nevada classic 1017 miles. Led the field by over two hours against the best cars and drivers that the West could produce; time 29 hours 43 minutes, with my Lincoln Road Runner; with a sealed radiator; never took on a drop of water.

Bill Bramlette

Bill Bramlette's 1,000 mile run received considerable press coverage in newspapers in California and Nevada.

17

The original Lincoln radiator emblem was silver-plated and identified the marque as "Leland-Built Lincoln".

Following Ford's purchase of Lincoln Motor Company, the radiator emblem was nickel-plated and identified the marque as "Ford Lincoln Detroit".

Two views of 1923 Fleetwood Model 2493 Landaulets.

A 1923 Phaeton with custom body by Guider-Sweetland Company, Detroit. Note removable solid "California" top and tonneau windshield.

Edsel Ford's personal 1923 Coupe with custom body by an unspecified coachbuilder, possibly Judkins.

A 1923 Model 126 Five-Passenger Coupe.

A 1923 cabriolet with custom coachwork by Holbrook.

A 1923 Brunn Model 117 Seven-Passenger Sedan.

The rear interior of a 1923 custom-bodied Brunn limousine.

A 1923 Brunn Model 123A Four-Passenger Phaeton, successor to the Model 112, at right.

A 1923 Brunn Model 112 Four-Passenger DeLuxe Phaeton.

A 1924 Brunn Model 123A Four-Passenger Phaeton.

Rear interior of a 1924 Brunn Model 123A Four-Passenger Phaeton. Note the side curtains and hardware stored beneath the rear cowl.

A 1924 Judkins Model 140A Two-Window Berline.

A 1924 Judkins Model 140C Three-Window Berline.

Another 1924 Judkins Model 140A Two-Window Berline.

Another 1924 Judkins Model 140C Three-Window Berline.

A 1924 Brunn Model 124B Seven-Passenger Touring.

A 1924 Brunn Model 130 Two-Passenger Roadster.

A 1924 Fleetwood Model 2340 Seven-Passenger Enclosed Drive Limousine.

The year is presumed to be 1924, although notes on the back of this photo identified the car as possibly a 1922 or 1923 Model 119. It *is* a Fleetwood Seven-Passenger Enclosed Drive Limousine.

A 1924 Brunn Model 135 Seven-Passenger Limousine.

A 1924 Judkins Model 702 Two-Passenger Coupe.

Two 1924 Brunn Model 126 Four-Passenger Coupes.

A 1924 Brunn Model 124 Seven-Passenger Touring.

A 1926 Dietrich Model 147A Seven-Passenger Sedan or Model 147B Seven-Passenger Berline.

A view of the interior of a 1926 Dietrich Model 146 Five-Passenger Sedan. Note the wicker door panel.

Another interior, this time the rear compartment of a Holbrook Cabriolet.

A 1926 Holbrook Model 153A Five-Passenger Collapsible Cabriolet. This New York Automobile Salon entrant was painted in colors supplied by Ditzler—Trogon Bronze Green and Raven Black with Derby Red striping. Inspiration was the Ecuadorian Golden-Headed Trogon.

A 1927 Locke Model 163B Four-Passenger Dual Cowl Sport Phaeton.

A 1927 Locke Model 151 Two-Passenger Roadster.

The J. B. Judkins Company stand at the 22nd Annual New York Automobile Salon featured this spectacular 1927 Model L, with Coaching Brougham coachwork.

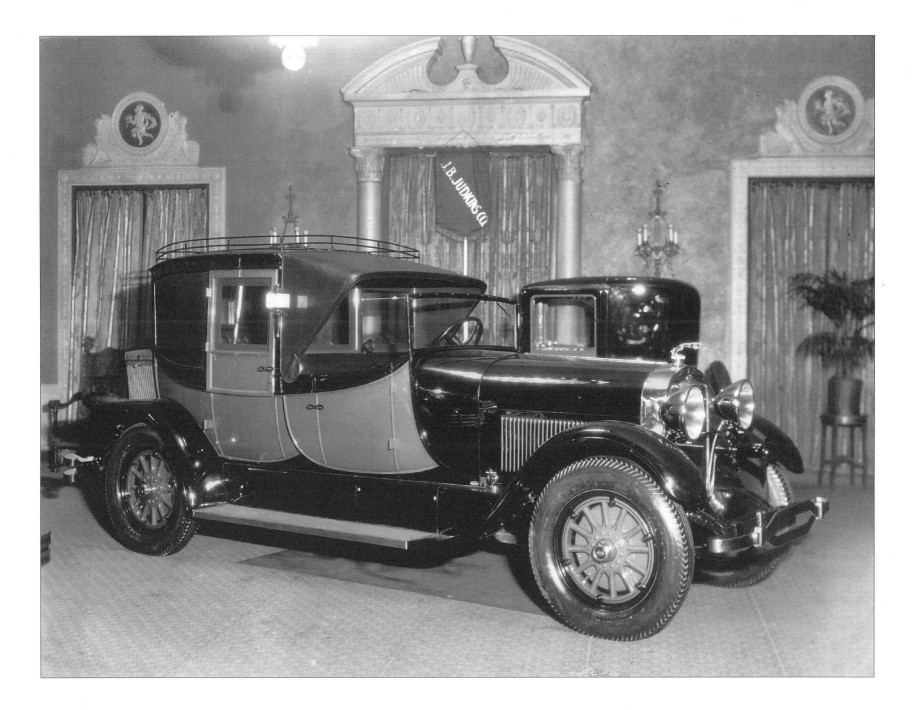

A 1927 Dietrich Model 147A Seven-Passenger Sedan.

A cutaway of the 384.8 cubic-inch V-8
Model L engine introduced in 1928.

A 1928 Judkins Model 170 Two-Passenger Sport Coupe.

A 1928 Locke Model 163B Four-Passenger Dual Cowl Sport Phaeton with right-hand drive.

A 1929 Model 179 Four-Passenger Coupe.

Thomas Edison, far right, and President Herbert Hoover aboard a 1925/26 Seven-Passenger Phaeton. The photo was taken in 1929.

Locke-designed and Locke-built, 1929 Model 164A
Seven-Passenger Sport Touring.

The 1929 LeBaron Aero Sport Phaeton, with polished aluminum body and bright green fenders. Note tailfin! The hit of the 1928 New York Automobile Salon, its instruments included an altimeter.

A 1930 Judkins Model 172 Two-Window Four-Passenger Berline.

From paper to pavement, the handsome 1930 Derham Model 189 Five-Passenger Convertible Phaeton.

A 1930 Dietrich Model 181 Four-Passenger Convertible Coupe.

Models K (V-8), KA, and KB
1931 through 1934

A 1931 K Judkins Model 218 Two-Passenger Coupe.

A 1931 K LeBaron Model 214 Two/Four-Passenger Convertible Roadster.

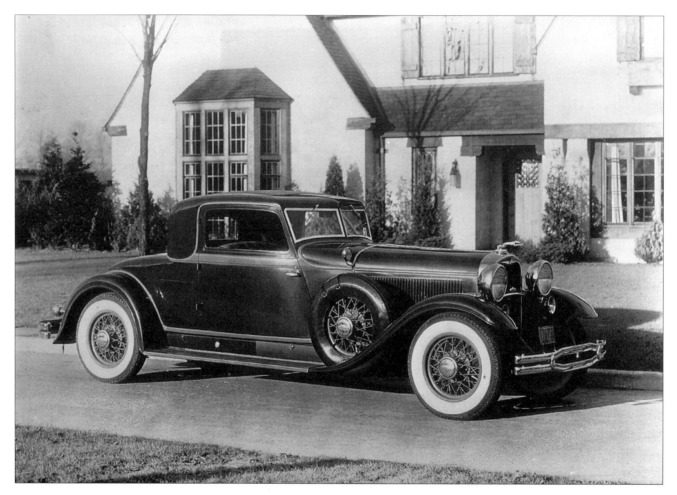

A 1931 K Dietrich Model 219 Two-Passenger Coupe.

A 1931 K custom sedan with coachwork by either Judkins or Dietrich.

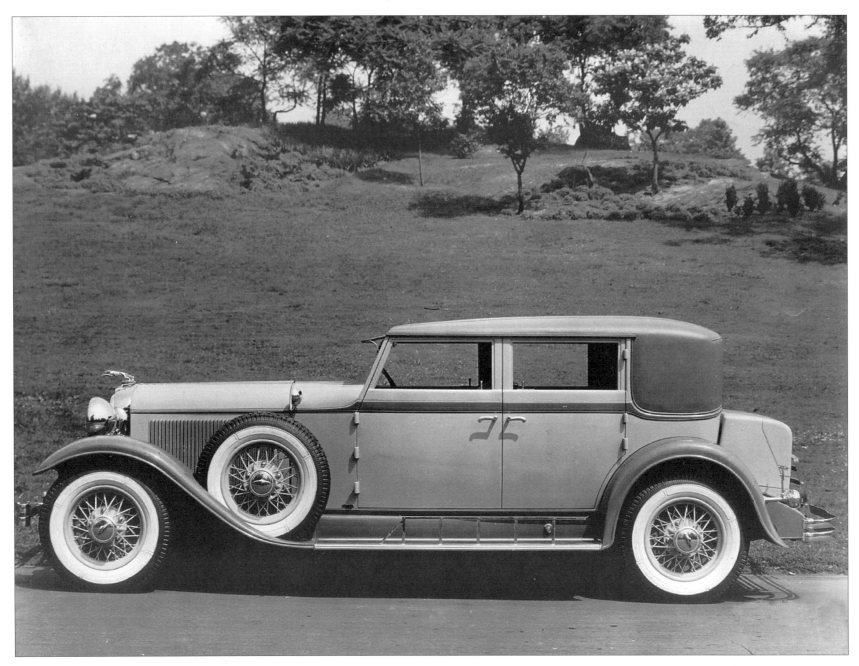

A 1931 K Rollston Town Sedan.

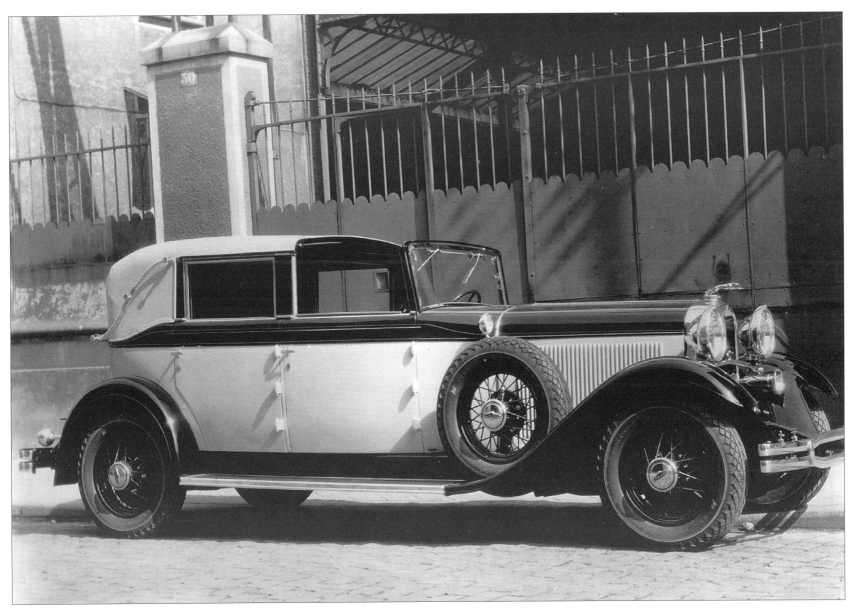

A 1931 K Million-Guiet Landaulet on the streets of Paris.

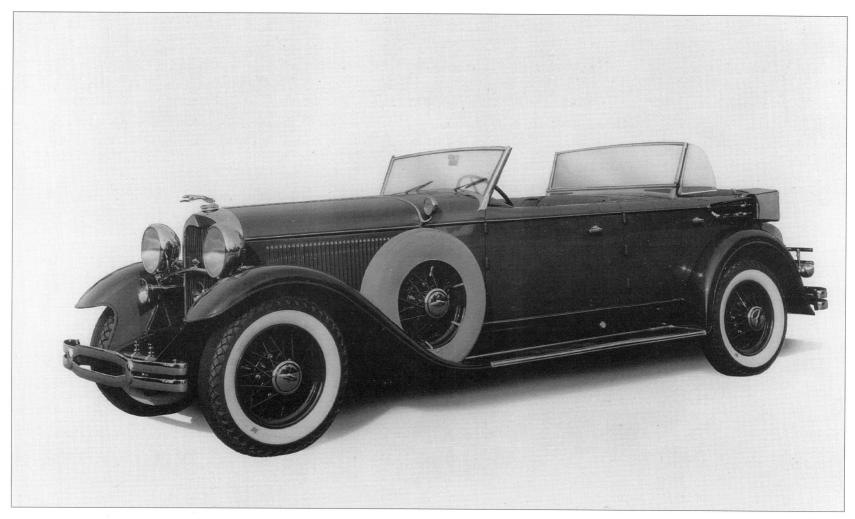

An exquisite K 1931 Murphy Dual Cowl Phaeton.

A 1931 K Murphy Two-Window Sedan.

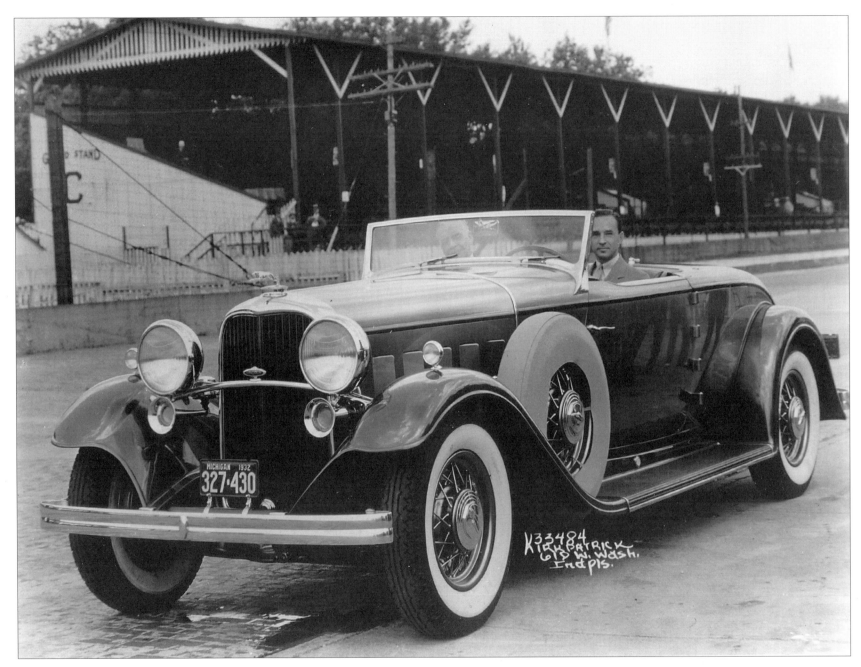

Edsel Ford at the wheel of the 1932 Indianapolis 500 pace car, a KB Murphy Model 248 Two/Four-Passenger Convertible Roadster.

Rear view of a KB Murphy Model 248 Two/Four-Passenger Convertible Roadster.

One of three KB Murphy Model 249 Two-Passenger Sport Roadsters.

Wrapped in KODAPAK and ready for delivery, a 1932 K-Series Seven-Passenger Sedan. In the background is a KB Brunn "Double Entry" Four-Passenger Sport Sedan.

More common than the Murphy roadsters but a classic nonetheless, a 1932 KB LeBaron Two/Four-Passenger Convertible Roadster.

A 1932 KB Dietrich Model 242B Two-Passenger Coupe.

A 1932 KB Brunn "Double Entry" Four-Passenger Sport Sedan.

A 1932 KB Brunn Four-Passenger Phaeton.

The Lincoln stand at the 33rd Annual New York Automobile Salon, Grand Central Palace, January 1933. To the right of the chassis is a KA Model 514B Five-Passenger Town Sedan; two places to its right is a KB Model 252A Four-Passenger Dual Cowl Sport Phaeton.

A 1933 KB Judkins Model 263A Four-Passenger Three-Window Berline.

Comedian W.C. Fields and a 1933 KB LeBaron Model 267B Two/Four Passenger Convertible Roadster.

A 1933 KA Model 514 Five-Passenger Town Sedan.

A 1934 LeBaron Two-Passenger Coupe on a KB chassis.

K-Series (V-12)
1935 through 1939

A 1935 Model 303A Seven-Passenger Three-Window Sedan on a 145-inch chassis.

Custom coachwork from Brunn, a 1935 Phaeton on a136-inch chassis.

A 1935 LeBaron Model 546 Five-Passenger Convertible Sedan on a 136-inch chassis.

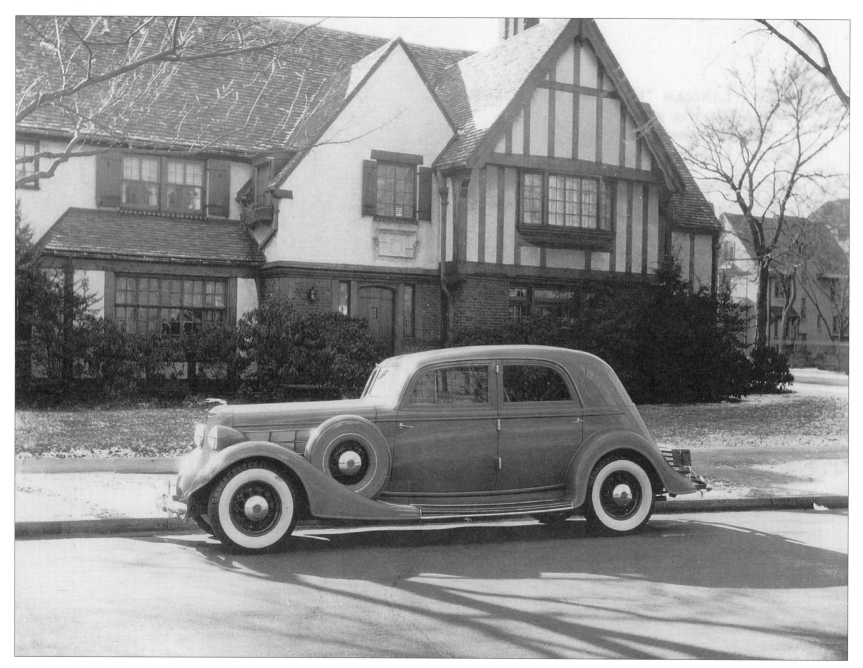

One of five 1935 Willoughby Model 311 Five-Passenger Sport Sedans on a 145-inch chassis.

A series of 1960s vintage photographs follow of Lucky Luciano's custom-built K roadster. Neither the year nor coachbuilder are identified.

The passenger compartment of the Lucky Luciano Lincoln.

A 1937 Brunn Model 359A Five-Passenger Non-Collapsible Cabriolet.

A 1937 Brunn Model 375 Five-Passenger Touring Cabriolet on a 145-inch chassis.

A 1938 Willoughby Five-Passenger Panel Brougham on a 145-inch chassis.

A 1938 LeBaron Five-Passenger Convertible Sedan on a 145-inch chassis.

Custom coachwork from Judkins on a 1938 chassis, a Four-Passenger Coupe.

A 1938 Brunn Model 425B Five-Passenger Touring Cabriolet on a 145-inch chassis.

A 1938 Model 404B Five-Passenger Three-Window Sedan.

One-of-a-kind, 1939 Willoughby Model 403 Seven-Passenger Touring.

Zephyr 1936 through 1942

Lincoln introduces the Zephyr to an appreciative audience.

The Zephyr unit/body frame, one of the first.

A 1936 Model 902 Six-Passenger Four-Door Sedan about to be loaded on a railcar.

On the road with a 1936 Model 902 Six-Passenger Four-Door Sedan.

New bumpers and a bit more chrome, a 1937 Model 730 Six-Passenger Four-Door Sedan.

The one-off 1938 Brunn Town Brougham.

At the 1938 Detroit Auto Show, a 1938 Model 720 Three-Passenger Coupe among the Zephyrs, Model Ks, and, in the distance, Packards and a bevy of Studebakers.

A 1939 Model H-73 Five-Passenger Sedan.

Nearing the finish of a grueling 306.5 mile economy run, a 1940 Zephyr stands for a glimpse of Yosemite Valley.

Artist's rendering of a 1941 Model 31 Custom Seven-Passenger Sedan.

Artist's rendering of a 1941 Model 32 Custom Seven-Passenger Limousine.

The front end of the 1942 Lincoln carried a massive steel grille across the full width of the car. The emblem above the name plate was a coat-of-arms adapted from the crest once borne by the Lincolns of Old England.

Continental 1940 through 1942

A 1940 Zephyr Model H56 "Continental" Five-Passenger Cabriolet.

Lincoln Continental script first appeared in 1941.

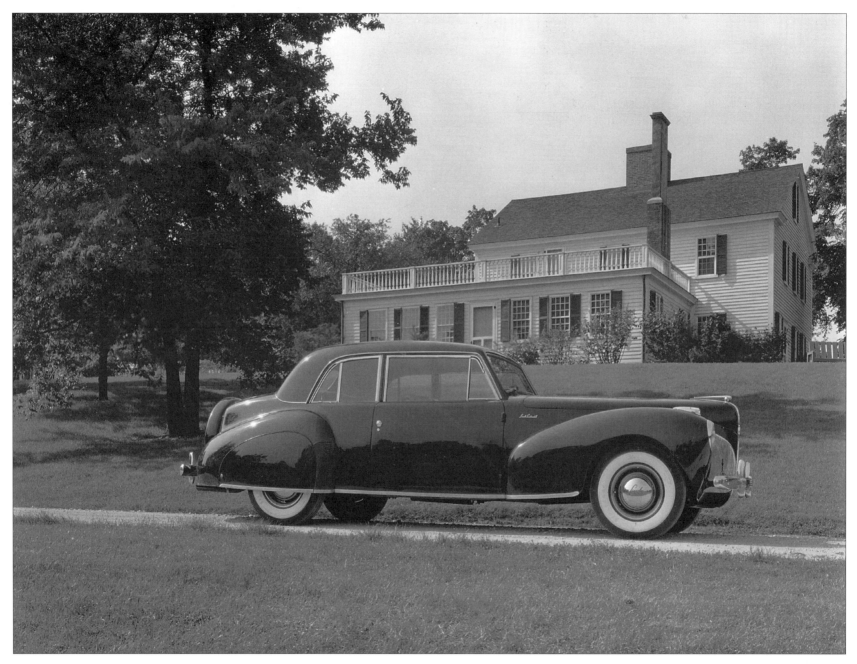

A 1941 Continental Model 57 Five-Passenger Coupe.

Admiring glances in the direction of a 1942 Model 56 Five-Passenger Cabriolet.

The Iconografix Photo Archive Series includes:

The Iconografix Photo Archive Series is available from direct mail specialty book dealers and bookstores worldwide, or can be ordered from the publisher. For additional information or to add your name to our mailing list contact:

Iconografix
PO Box 609/BK
Osceola, Wisconsin 54020 USA

Telephone: (715) 294-2792
(800) 289-3504 (USA)
Fax: (715) 294-3414

U.S. book trade distribution by Voyageur Press, Inc., PO Box 338, Stillwater, Minnesota 55082 (800) 888-9653
European distribution by Midland Publishing Limited, 24 The Hollow, Earl Shilton, Leicester LE9 7N1 England

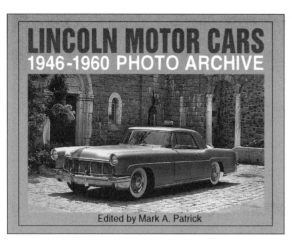

MORE GREAT BOOKS FROM ICONOGRAFIX

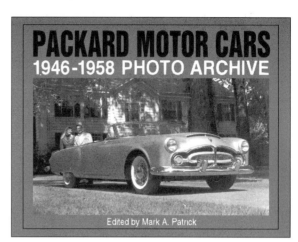

LINCOLN MOTOR CARS 1946-1960 *Photo Archive* ISBN 1-882256-58-1

PACKARD MOTOR CARS 1946-1958 *Photo Archive* ISBN 1-882256-45-X

IMPERIAL 1955-1963 *Photo Archive* ISBN 1-882256-22-0

STUDEBAKER 1946-1958 *Photo Archive* ISBN 1-882256-25-5

DODGE TRUCKS 1948-1960 *Photo Archive* ISBN 1-882256-37-9

COCA-COLA: A HISTORY IN PHOTO-GRAPHS 1930-1969 *Photo Archive* ISBN 1-882256-46-8

AMERICAN SERVICE STATIONS 1935-1943 *Photo Archive* ISBN 1-882256-27-1

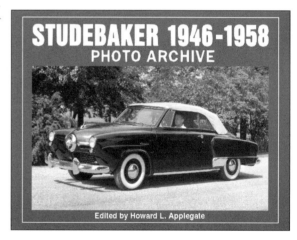

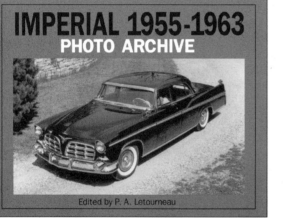

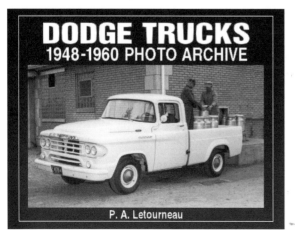

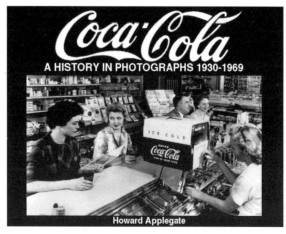

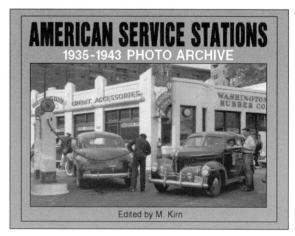